ADVANCED PIANO SOLOS
ENCYCLOPEDIA
VOL. 1

ARRANGED BY
TOM ROED

FEATURING THE BEST IN
POPS • MOVIE • BROADWAY • JAZZ
LOVE SONGS • TV • COUNTRY

Alfred Music
P.O. Box 10003
Van Nuys, CA 91410-0003
alfred.com

ISBN-10: 0-7579-9530-6
ISBN-13: 978-0-7579-9530-9

Cover Design: Odalis Soto

CONTENTS

All For Love 24

All I Have. 38

Big Spender 42

(They Long To Be) Close To You. 35

Didn't We Almost Have It All 28

Don't Get Around Much Anymore 114

Don't Wanna Lose You 32

Europa (Earth's Cry Heaven's Smile). 46

Evergreen 12

Forever's As Far As I'll Go 18

Funeral March Of A Marionette 108

Have You Ever Really Loved A Woman? 52

I Honestly Love You 55

I Swear. 9

If Ever You're In My Arms Again 58

If You Say My Eyes Are Beautiful. 128

I'll Be There For You 98

Jeopardy Theme. 106

Johnny's Theme. 104

The Lady In Red 21

Linus And Lucy 62

The Lion Sleeps Tonight. 154

Midnight Creepin' 150

My Way 116

On The Wings Of Love. 68

The Pink Panther. 132

Proud Mary. 74

Right Here Waiting 91

The Rose 4

Searchin' My Soul 94

Steam Heat 111

Take Five 78

Taking A Chance On Love 82

Theme From Ice Castles (Through The Eyes Of Love). 88

Tonight, I Celebrate My Love 85

Unanswered Prayers. .138

Up Where We Belong. .134

We've Only Just Begun 142

When The Night Comes 146

You Light Up My Life 158

You Stepped Out Of A Dream 121

You're The Inspiration .124

CONTENTS BY CATEGORY

COUNTRY

Title	Page No.
All I Have	38
Forever's As Far As I'll Go	18
I Swear	9
Unanswered Prayers	138

JAZZ

Title	Page No.
Don't Get Around Much Anymore	114
Europa (Earth's Cry Heaven's Smile)	46
Midnight Creepin'	150
Take Five	78
Taking A Chance On Love	82
You Stepped Out Of A Dream	121

LOVE SONGS

Title	Page No.
Don't Wanna Lose You	32
I Honestly Love You	55
If You Say My Eyes Are Beautiful	128
On The Wings Of Love	68
Right Here Waiting	91
The Lady In Red	21
Tonight, I Celebrate My Love	85
We've Only Just Begun	142

BROADWAY AND MOVIE SONGS

Title		Page No.
All For Love	THE THREE MUSKETEERS	24
Big Spender	SWEET CHARITY	42
Evergreen	A STAR IS BORN	12
Have You Ever Really Loved A Woman?	DON JUAN DeMARCO	52
The Lion Sleeps Tonight	THE LION KING	154
The Pink Panther	THE PINK PANTHER	132
The Rose	THE ROSE	4
Steam Heat	PAJAMA GAME	111
Theme From Ice Castles (Through The Eyes Of Love)	ICE CASTLES	88
Up Where We Belong	AN OFFICER AND A GENTLEMAN	134
You Light Up My Life	YOU LIGHT UP MY LIFE	158

POP

Title	Page No.
(They Long To Be) Close To You	35
Didn't We Almost Have It All	28
If Ever You're In My Arms Again	58
My Way	116
Proud Mary	74
When The Night Comes	146
You're The Inspiration	124

TV

Title		Page No.
Funeral March Of A Marionette	ALFRED HITCHCOCK PRESENTS	108
I'll Be There For You	FRIENDS	98
Jeopardy Theme	JEOPARDY!	106
Johnny's Theme	THE TONIGHT SHOW	104
Linus And Lucy	PEANUTS™ TV SPECIALS	62
Searchin' My Soul	ALLY McBEAL	94

From the Twentieth Century-Fox Motion Picture "THE ROSE"

THE ROSE

Words and Music by
AMANDA McBROOM
Arranged by TOM ROED

I SWEAR

Words and Music by
GARY BAKER and FRANK MYERS
Arranged by TOM ROED

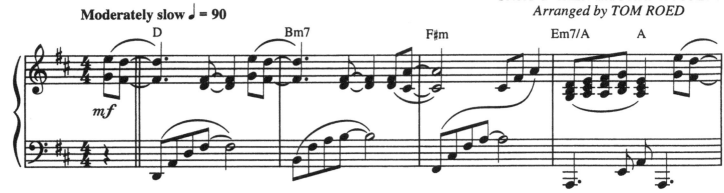

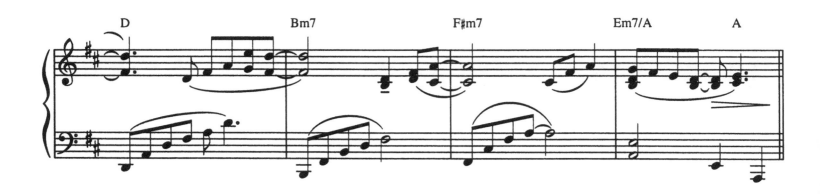

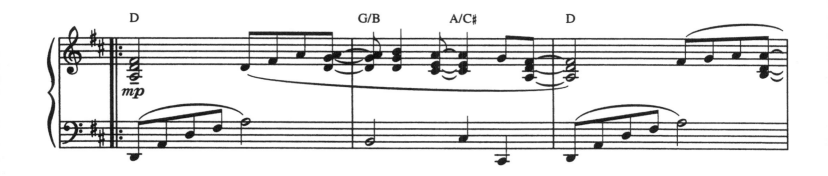

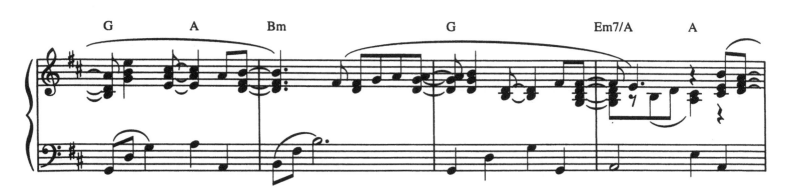

I Swear - 3 - 1
AR004

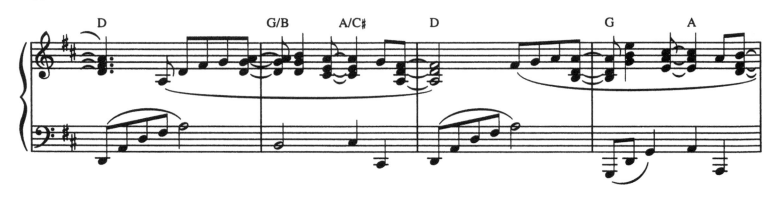

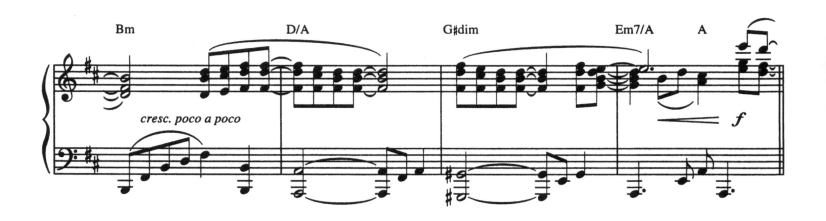

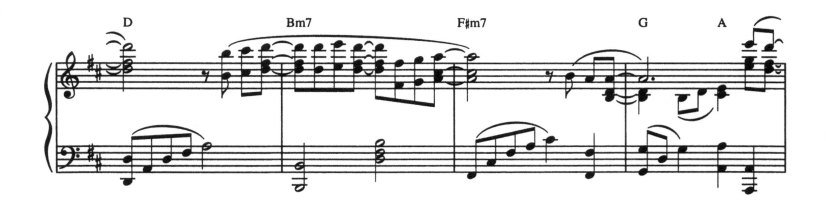

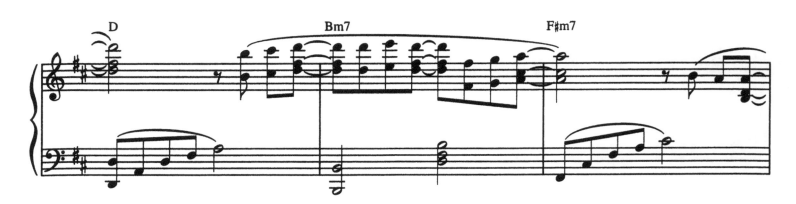

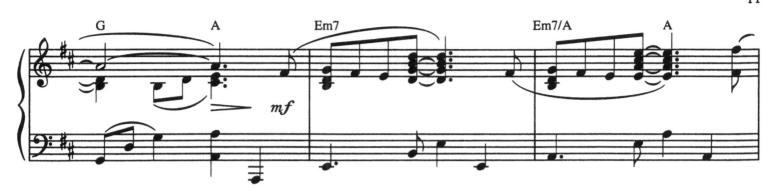

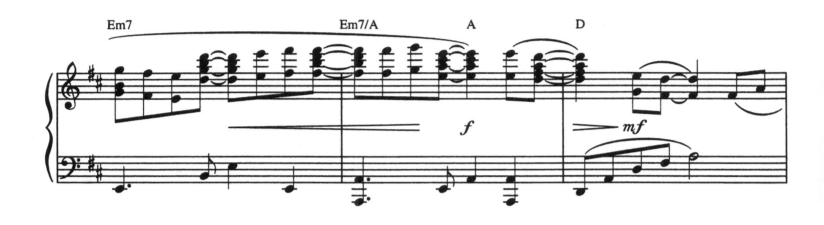

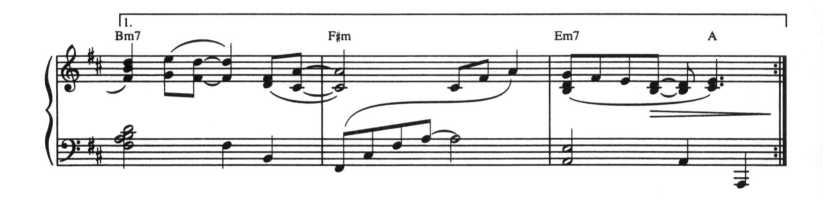

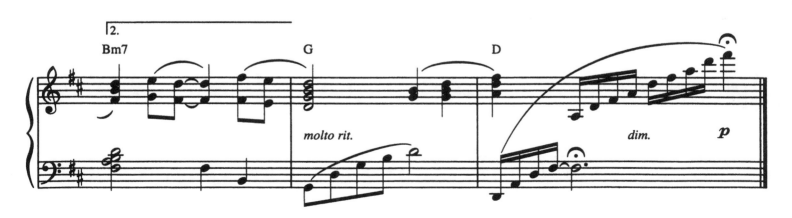

Love Theme from "A STAR IS BORN"

EVERGREEN

Words by PAUL WILLIAMS

Music by BARBRA STREISAND
Arranged by TOM ROED

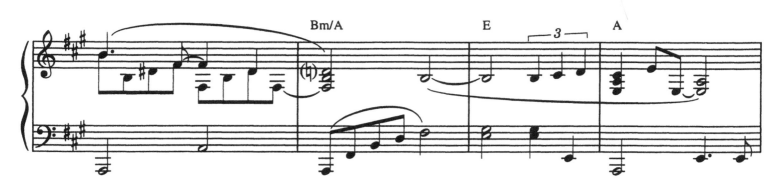

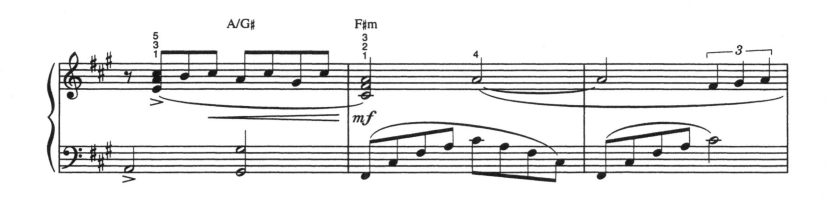

Evergreen - 6 - 2

FOREVER'S AS FAR AS I'LL GO

Words and Music by
MIKE REID
Arranged by TOM ROED

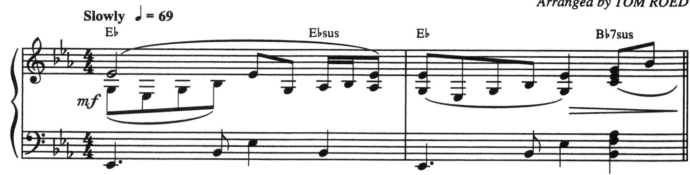

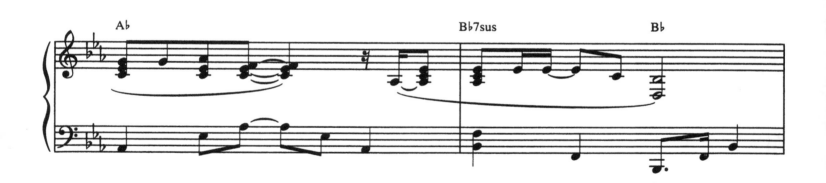

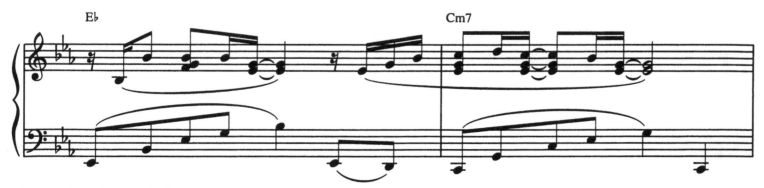

Forever's As Far As I'll Go - 3 - 1
AR004

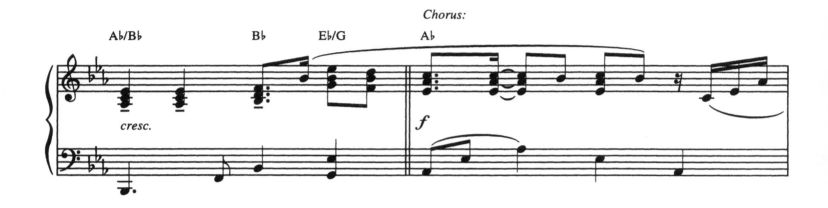

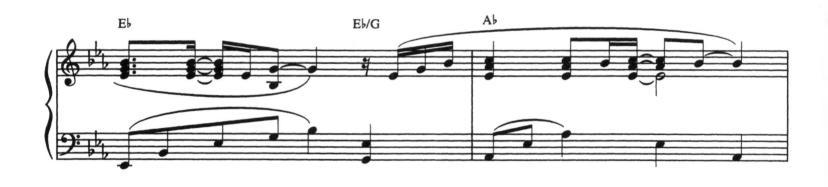

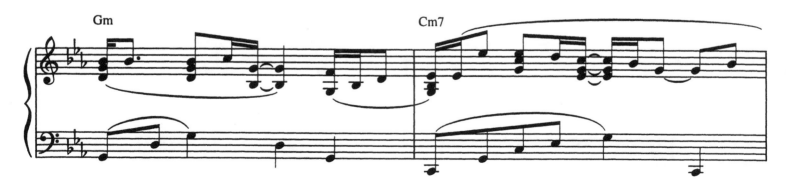

THE LADY IN RED

By
CHRIS DeBURGH

The Lady In Red - 3 - 1

The Lady In Red - 3 - 3

From the Original Motion Picture Soundtrack "THE THREE MUSKETEERS"

ALL FOR LOVE

Written by
BRYAN ADAMS, ROBERT JOHN "MUTT" LANGE
and MICHAEL KAMEN
Arranged by TOM ROED

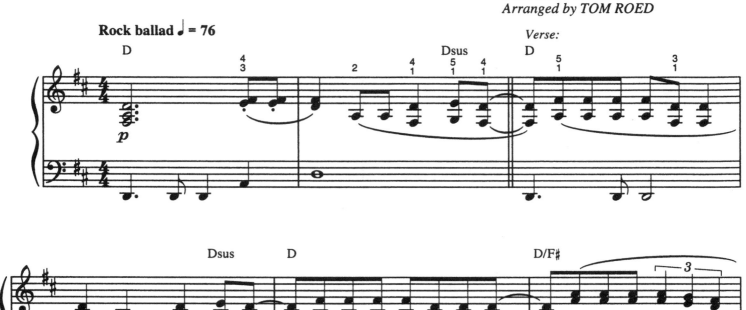

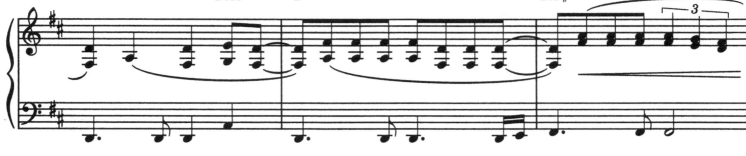

All for Love - 4 - 1
AR004

DIDN'T WE ALMOST HAVE IT ALL

By
MICHAEL MASSER and
WILL JENNINGS

Didn't We Almost Have It All - 4 - 1

Didn't We Almost Have It All - 4 - 2

Didn't We Almost Have It All - 4 - 4

DON'T WANNA LOSE YOU

Slow rock ballad ♩ = 80

Words and Music by
GLORIA ESTEFAN

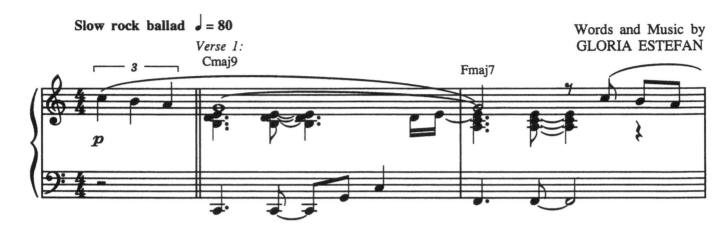

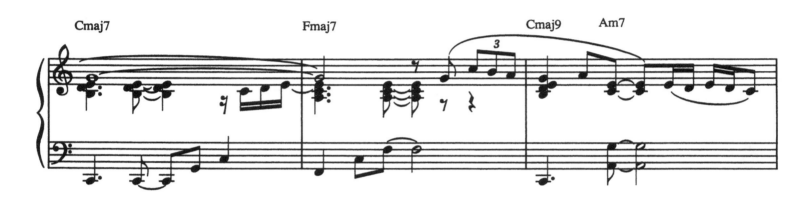

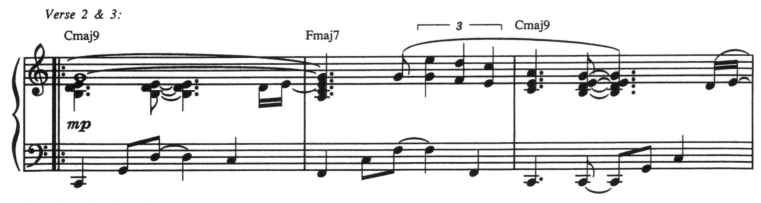

Don't Wanna Lose You - 3 - 1
AR004

* omit bottom note in right hand for easier playing

Don't Wanna Lose You - 3 - 2

(They Long To Be)
CLOSE TO YOU

Words by
HAL DAVID

Music by
BURT BACHARACH
Arranged by TOM ROED

Close To You - 3 - 1

ALL I HAVE

Words and Music by
BETH NIELSEN CHAPMAN and ERIC KAZ
Arranged by TOM ROED

Moderately slow ♩ = 72

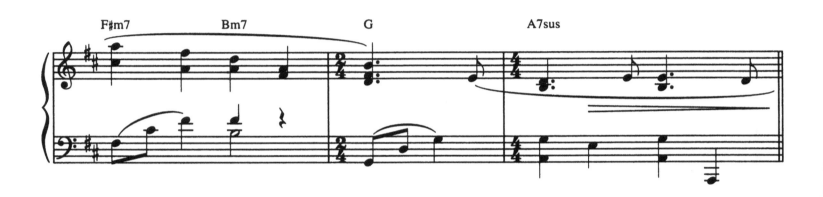

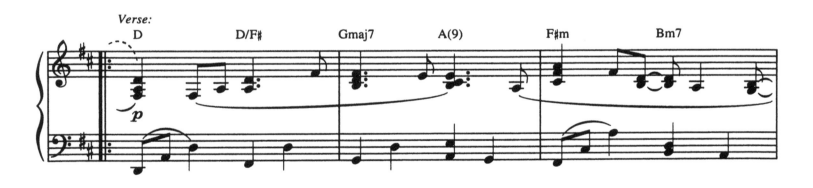

All I Have - 4 - 1
AR004

All I Have - 4 - 2

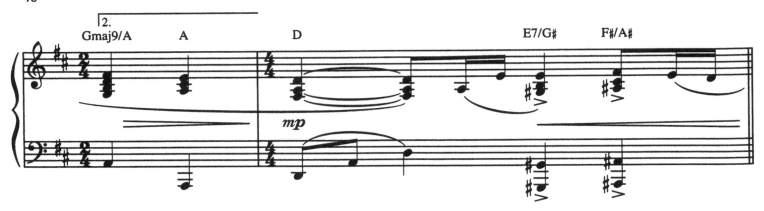

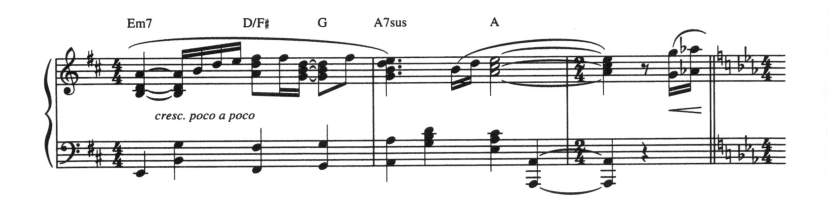

All I Have - 4 - 3

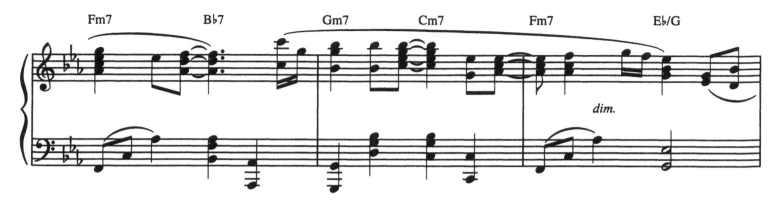

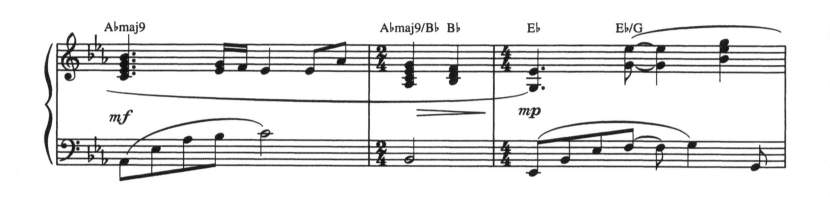

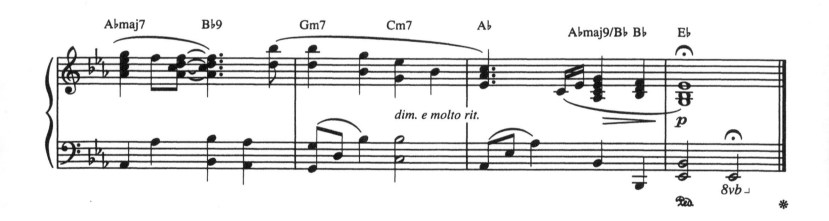

From the Musical Comedy "SWEET CHARITY"

BIG SPENDER

By
CY COLEMAN and
DOROTHY FIELDS

Big Spender - 4 - 1

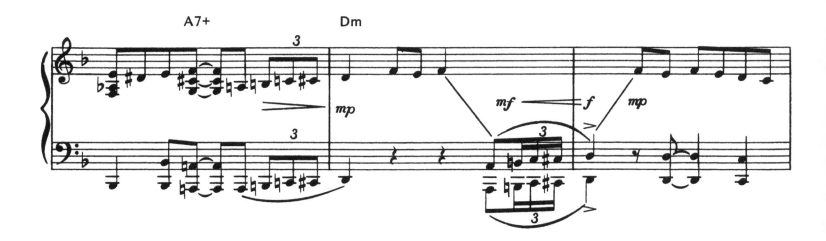

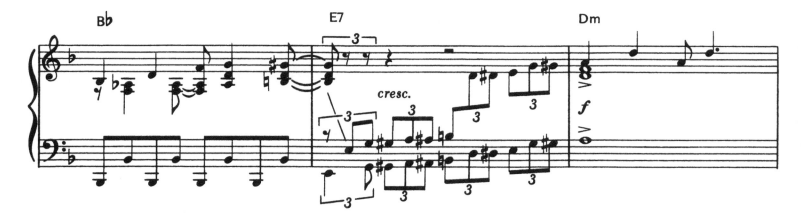

Big Spender - 4 - 2

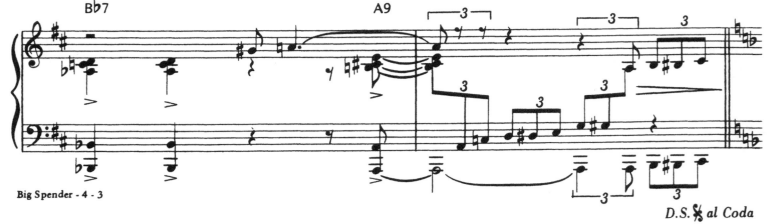

D.S. 𝄋 al Coda

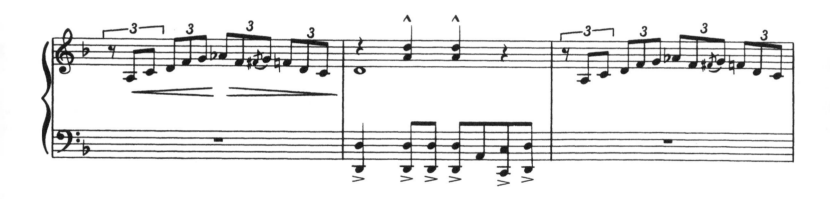

Big Spender - 4 - 4

EUROPA
(Earth's Cry Heaven's Smile)

By
CARLOS SANTANA
and TOM COSTER
Arranged by TOM ROED

From the Original Motion Picture Soundtrack "DON JUAN DeMARCO"

HAVE YOU EVER REALLY LOVED A WOMAN?

Lyrics by
BRYAN ADAMS and
ROBERT JOHN "MUTT" LANGE

Music by
MICHAEL KAMEN
Arranged by TOM ROED

I HONESTLY LOVE YOU

By
PETER ALLEN and
JEFF BARRY

I Honestly Love You - 3 - 1

IF EVER YOU'RE IN MY ARMS AGAIN

By MICHAEL MASSER,
TOM SNOW and CYNTHIA WEIL

If Ever You're In My Arms Again - 4 - 1

If Ever You're In My Arms Again - 4 - 2

If Ever You're In My Arms Again - 4 - 4

LINUS AND LUCY

By VINCE GUARALDI

Moderately Bright, with spirit ♩ = 138

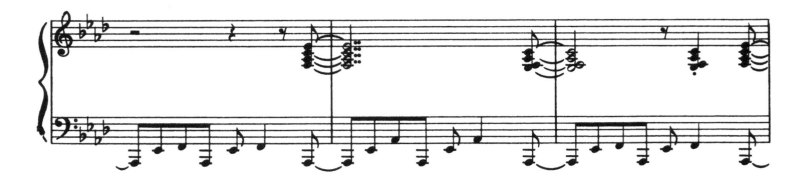

Linus And Lucy - 6 - 1

Linus And Lucy - 6 - 2

Linus And Lucy - 6 - 4

ON THE WINGS OF LOVE

By
JEFFREY OSBORNE
and PETER SCHLESS

On the Wings of Love - 6 - 1

On the Wings of Love - 6 - 2

On the Wings of Love - 6 - 4

PROUD MARY

By
J.C. FOGERTY

Proud Mary - 4 - 1

Proud Mary - 4 - 4

TAKE FIVE

By
PAUL DESMOND

Take Five - 4 - 1

Take Five - 4 - 2

Take Five - 4 - 4

From the M-G-M Musical Production "CABIN IN THE SKY"

TAKING A CHANCE ON LOVE

By
JOHN LATOUCHE, TED FETTER
and VERNON DUKE

Taking A Chance On Love - 3 - 1

TONIGHT I CELEBRATE MY LOVE

By
MICHAEL MASSER and
GERRY GOFFIN

Tonight I Celebrate My Love - 3 - 1
AR004

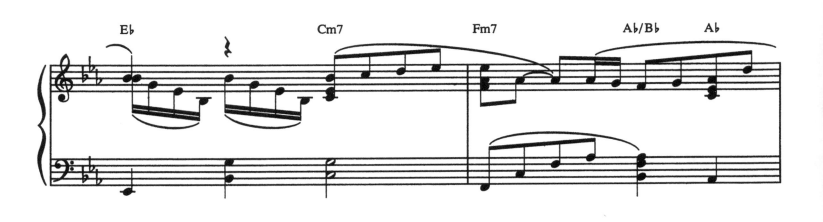

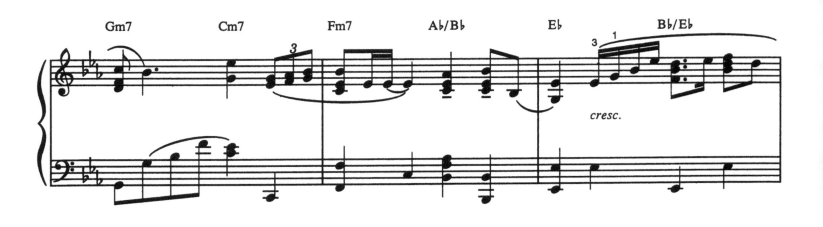

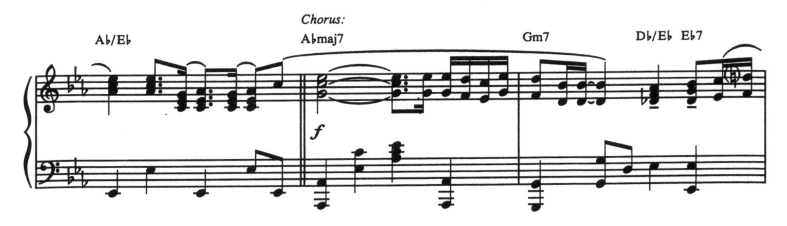

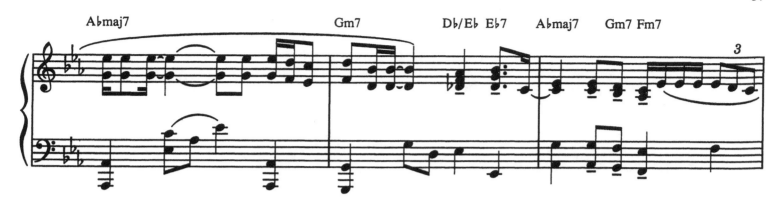

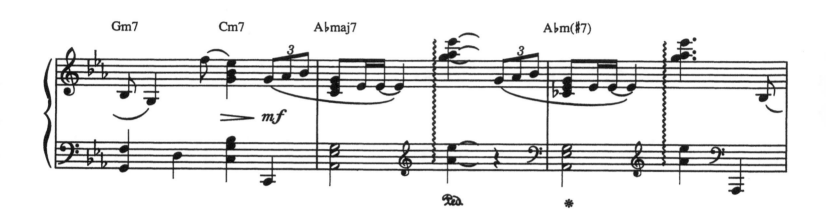

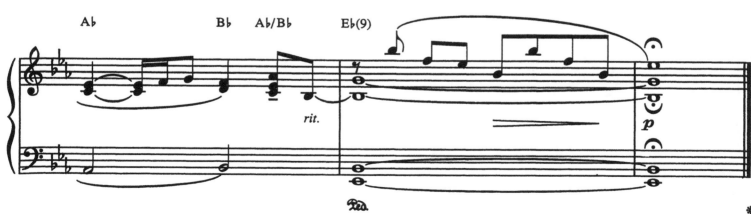

Tonight I Celebrate My Love - 3 - 3

From the Columbia Motion Picture "ICE CASTLES"

THEME FROM ICE CASTLES
(Through the Eyes of Love)

By
CAROLE BAYER SAGER and
MARVIN HAMLISCH

Slowly and very expressively ♩ = 76

Theme from Ice Castles - 3 - 1

Theme from Ice Castles - 3 - 2

RIGHT HERE WAITING

Words and Music by
RICHARD MARX
Arranged by TOM ROED

Moderately slow ♩ = 88

From the Twentieth Century Fox Television Series
Ally McBeal

SEARCHIN' MY SOUL

Words and Music by
VONDA SHEPARD and
HOWARD GORDON
Arranged by TOM ROED

Moderately bright ♩ = 112

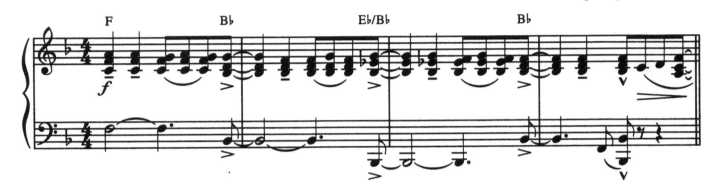

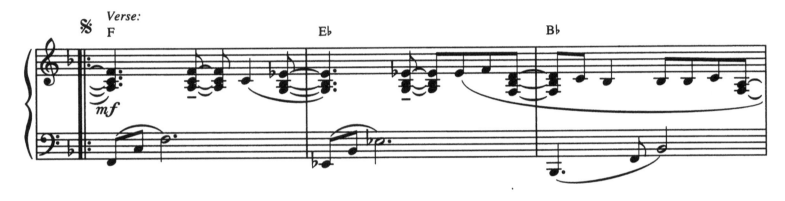

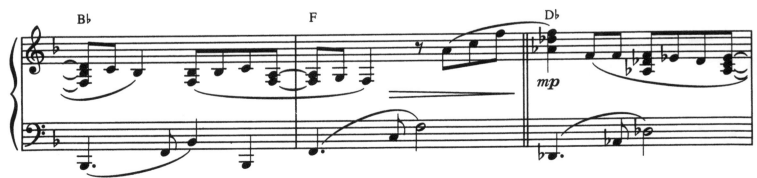

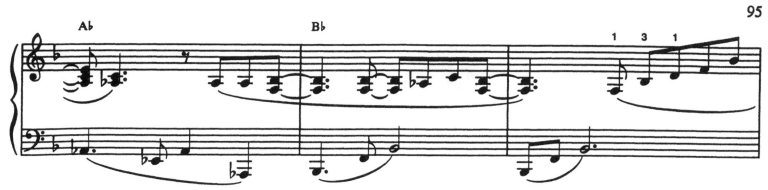

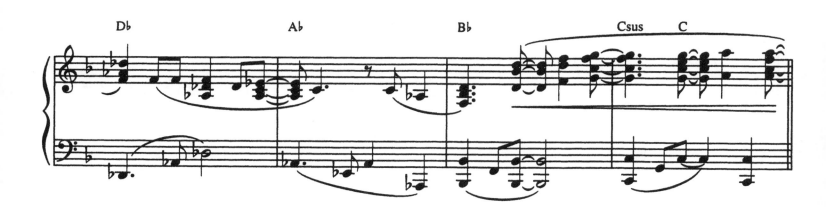

Chorus:

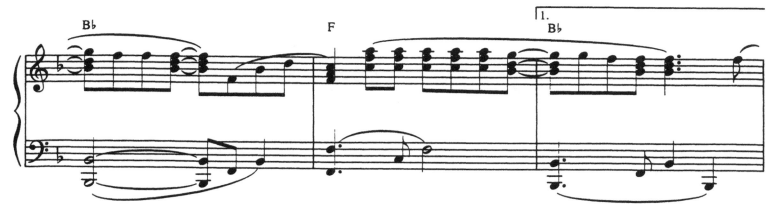

I'LL BE THERE FOR YOU
(Theme from "FRIENDS")

Words by
DAVID CRANE, MARTA KAUFFMAN, ALLEE WILLIS,
PHIL SOLEM and DANNY WILDE

Music by
MICHAEL SKLOFF
Arranged by TOM ROED

Fast rock ♩ = 190

I'll Be There for You - 6 - 1
AR004

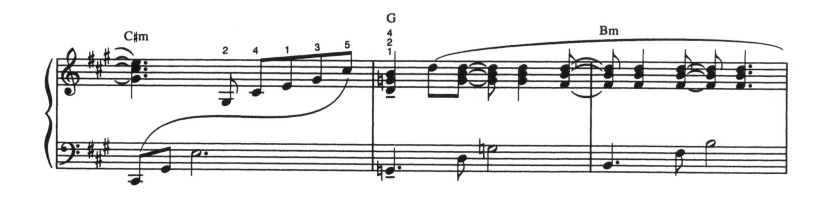

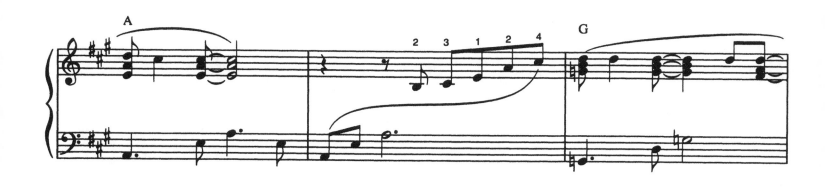

I'll Be There for You - 6 - 2

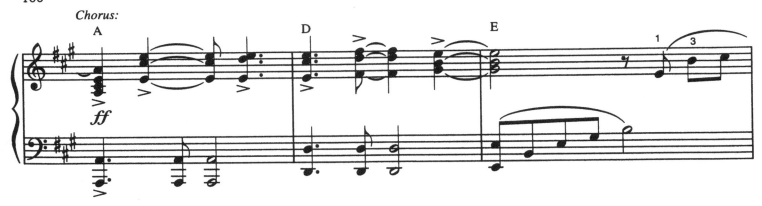

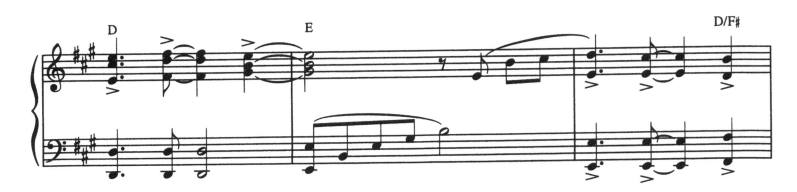

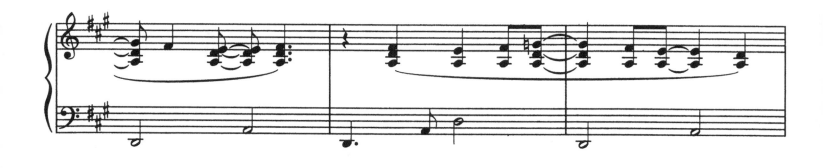

I'll Be There for You - 6 - 4

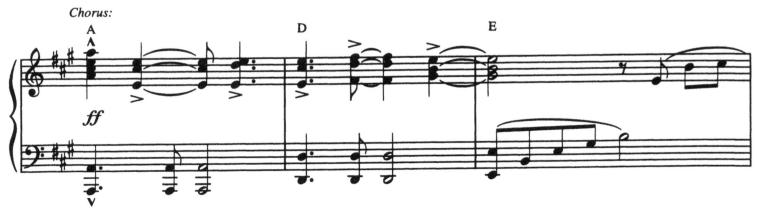

I'll Be There for You - 6 - 5

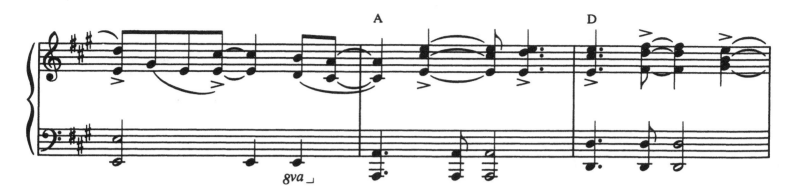

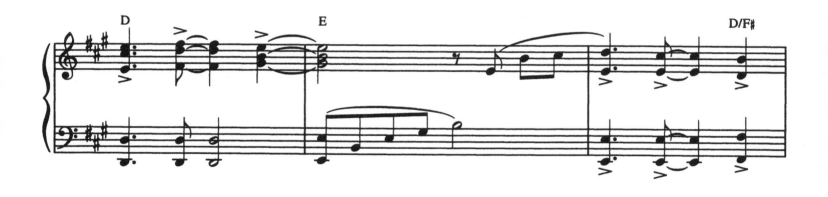

I'll Be There for You - 6 - 6

JOHNNY'S THEME

Music by PAUL ANKA
and JOHNNY CARSON
Arranged by TOM ROED

Johnny's Theme - 2 - 1
AR004

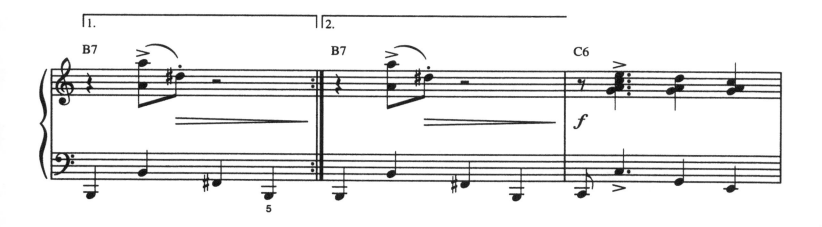

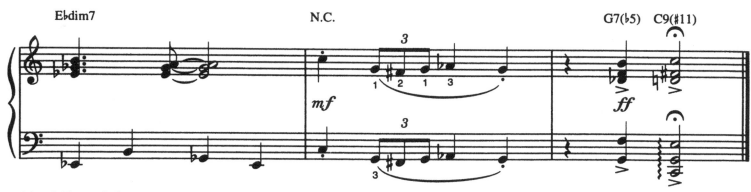

Johnny's Theme - 2 - 2

JEOPARDY THEME

Music by
MERV GRIFFIN

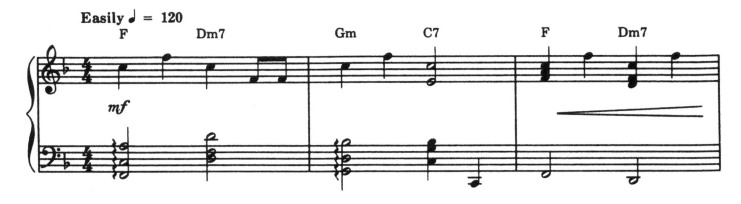

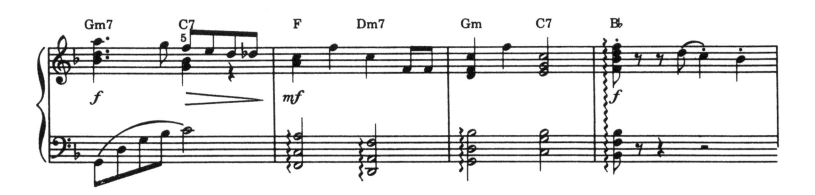

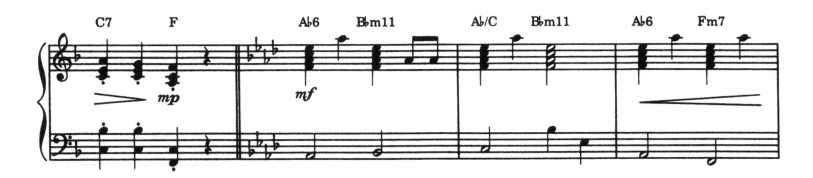

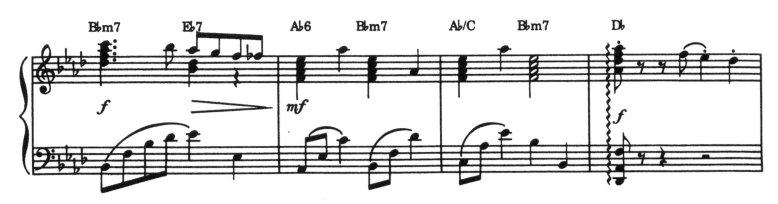

Jeopardy Theme - 2 - 1

Alfred Hitchcock Presents

FUNERAL MARCH OF A MARIONETTE

CHARLES GOUNOD
(1818 - 1893)

Funeral March Of A Marionette - 3 - 1

Funeral March Of A Marionette- 3 - 2

110

Funeral March Of A Marionette- 3 - 3

From the Broadway Musical Production "PAJAMA GAME"

STEAM HEAT

By
RICHARD ADLER and
JERRY ROSS

Steam Heat- 3 - 1

DON'T GET AROUND MUCH ANYMORE

By
BOB RUSSELL and
DUKE ELLINGTON

Don't Get Around Much Anymore - 2 - 1

Don't Get Around Much Anymore - 2 - 2

MY WAY

Original French Words by
GILES THIBAULT

English Words by PAUL ANKA
Music by JACQUES REVAUX
and CLAUDE FRANCOIS
Arranged by TOM ROED

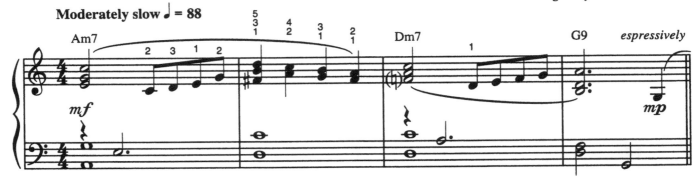

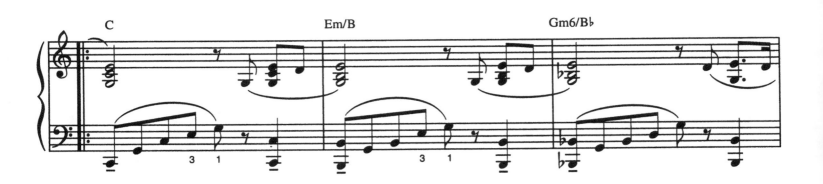

My Way - 5 - 1
AR004

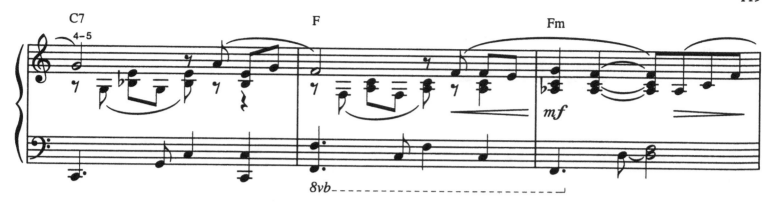

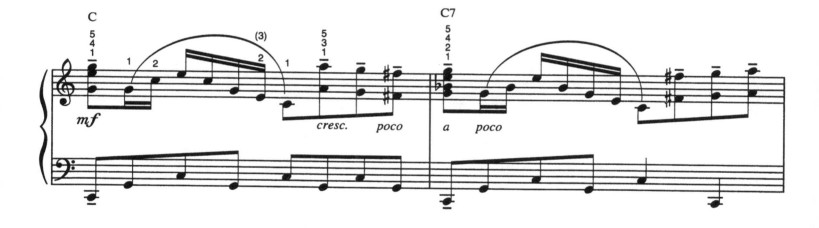

From the Metro-Goldwyn-Mayer Musical Production "ZIEGFELD GIRL"

YOU STEPPED OUT OF A DREAM

By
GUS KAHN and
NACIO HERB BROWN

You Stepped Out Of A Dream - 3 - 1

You Stepped Out Of A Dream - 3 - 2

YOU'RE THE INSPIRATION

Words and Music by
PETER CETERA and
DAVID FOSTER

You're The Inspiration - 4 - 1

You're The Inspiration - 4 - 4

IF YOU SAY MY EYES ARE BEAUTIFUL

By
ELLIOT WILLENSKY

If You Say My Eyes Are Beautiful - 4 - 1

130

If You Say My Eyes Are Beautiful - 4 - 3

If You Say My Eyes Are Beautiful - 4 - 4

Theme Song from the Mirisch-G&E Production, "THE PINK PANTHER," a United Artists Release

THE PINK PANTHER

Music by
HENRY MANCINI

The Pink Panther - 2 - 1

The Pink Panther - 2 - 2

Paramount Pictures Presents A Lorimar-Martin Elfand Production-A Taylor Hackford Film
"AN OFFICER AND A GENTLEMAN"

UP WHERE WE BELONG

By
WILL JENNINGS, BUFFY SAINTE-MARIE
and **JACK NITZSCHE**

136

Up Where We Belong - 4 - 3

Up Where We Belong - 4 - 4

UNANSWERED PRAYERS

Words and Music by
LARRY B. BASTIAN, PAT ALGER
and GARTH BROOKS
Arranged by TOM ROED

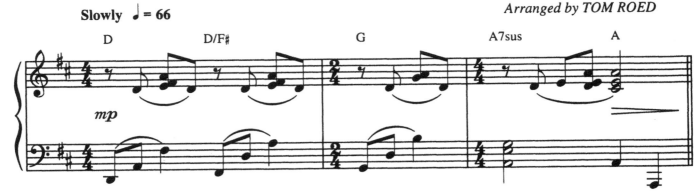

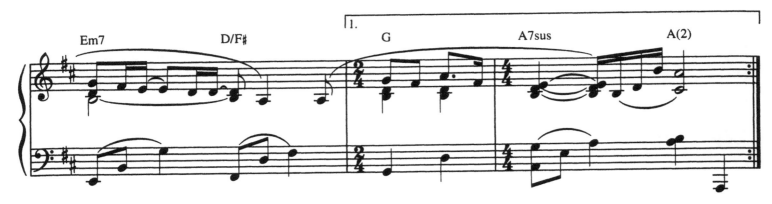

Unanswered Prayers - 4 - 1
AR004

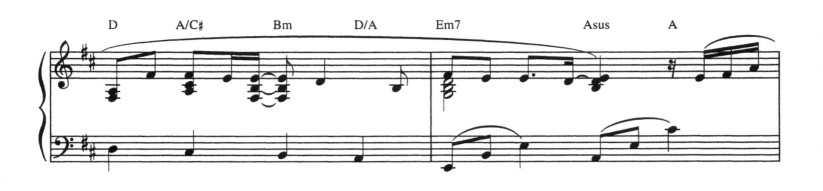

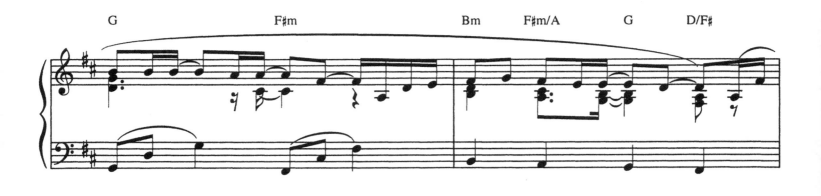

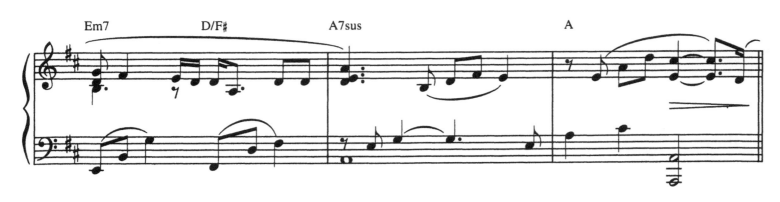

WE'VE ONLY JUST BEGUN

By
PAUL WILLIAMS and
ROGER NICHOLS

Slowly, tenderly ♩ = 72

We've Only Just Begun - 4 - 2

We've Only Just Begun - 4 - 4

WHEN THE NIGHT COMES

By
BRYAN ADAMS, JIM VALLANCE
& DIANE WARREN

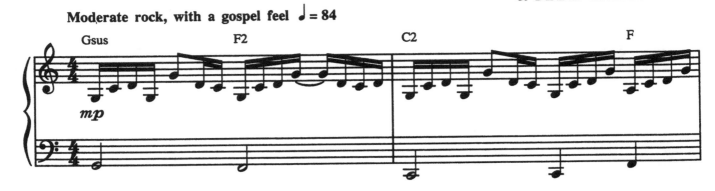

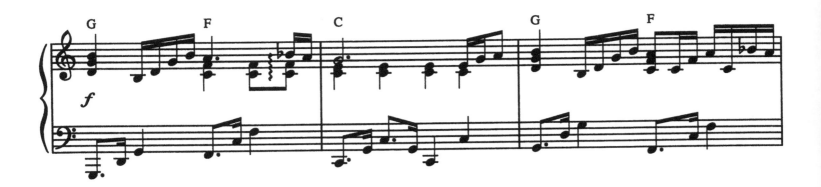

When The Night Comes - 4 - 1
AR004

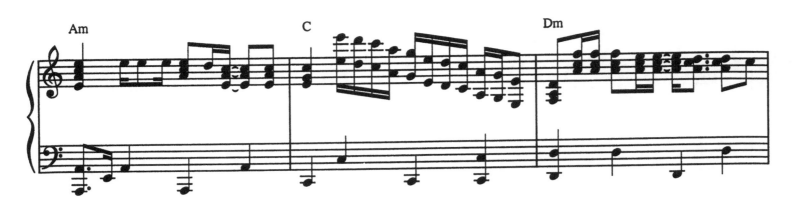

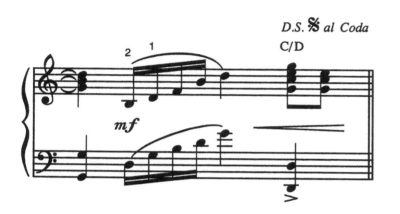

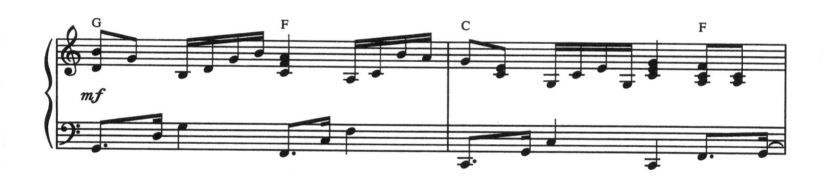

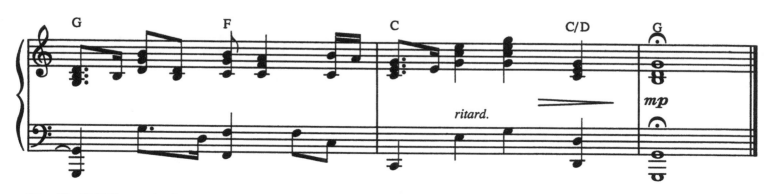

When The Night Comes - 4 - 4

MIDNIGHT CREEPIN'

By TOM ROED

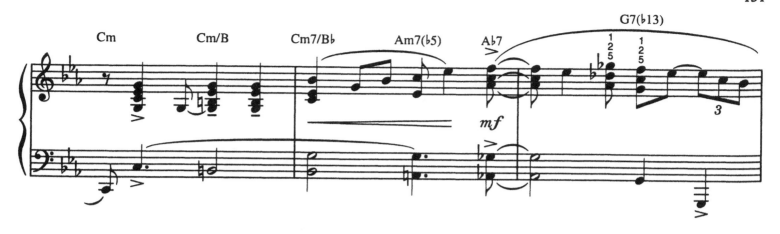

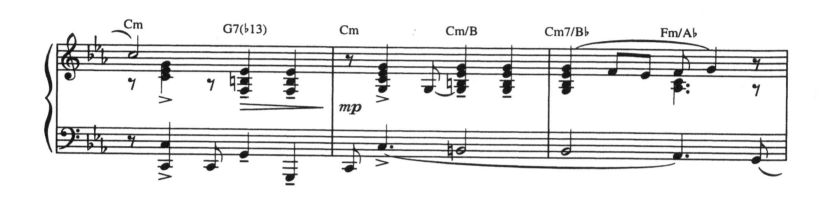

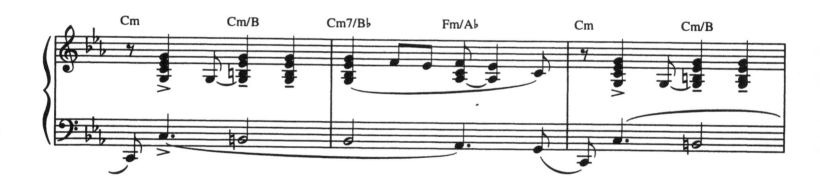

Midnight Creepin' - 4 - 2

Midnight Creepin' - 4 - 4

From the Motion Picture "THE LION KING"

THE LION SLEEPS TONIGHT

New Lyric and Revised Music by
GEORGE DAVID WEISS, HUGO PERETTI
and LUIGI CREATORE
Arranged by TOM ROED

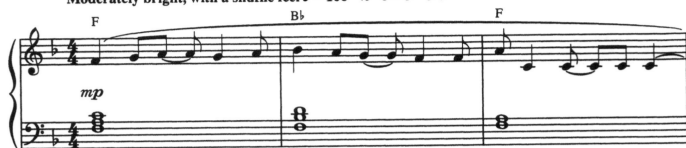

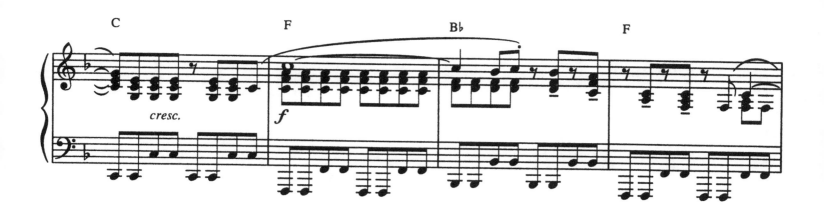

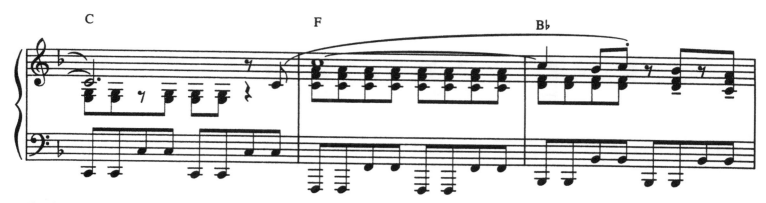

The Lion Sleeps Tonight - 4 - 2

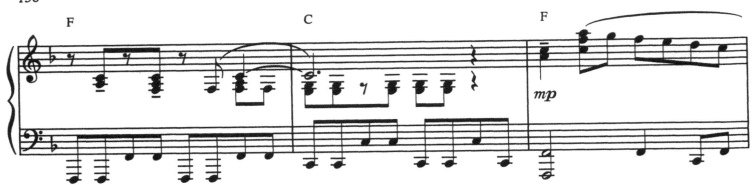

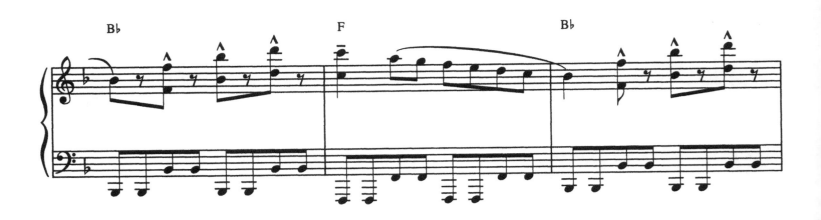

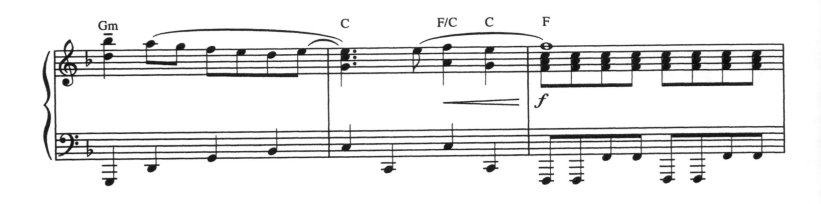

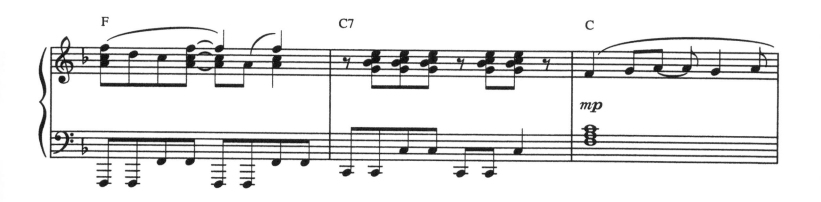

The Lion Sleeps Tonight - 4 - 4

From the Columbia Pictures Release ''YOU LIGHT UP MY LIFE''

YOU LIGHT UP MY LIFE

By
JOE BROOKS

You Light Up My Life - 3 - 1

You Light Up My Life - 3 - 2